CW01215595

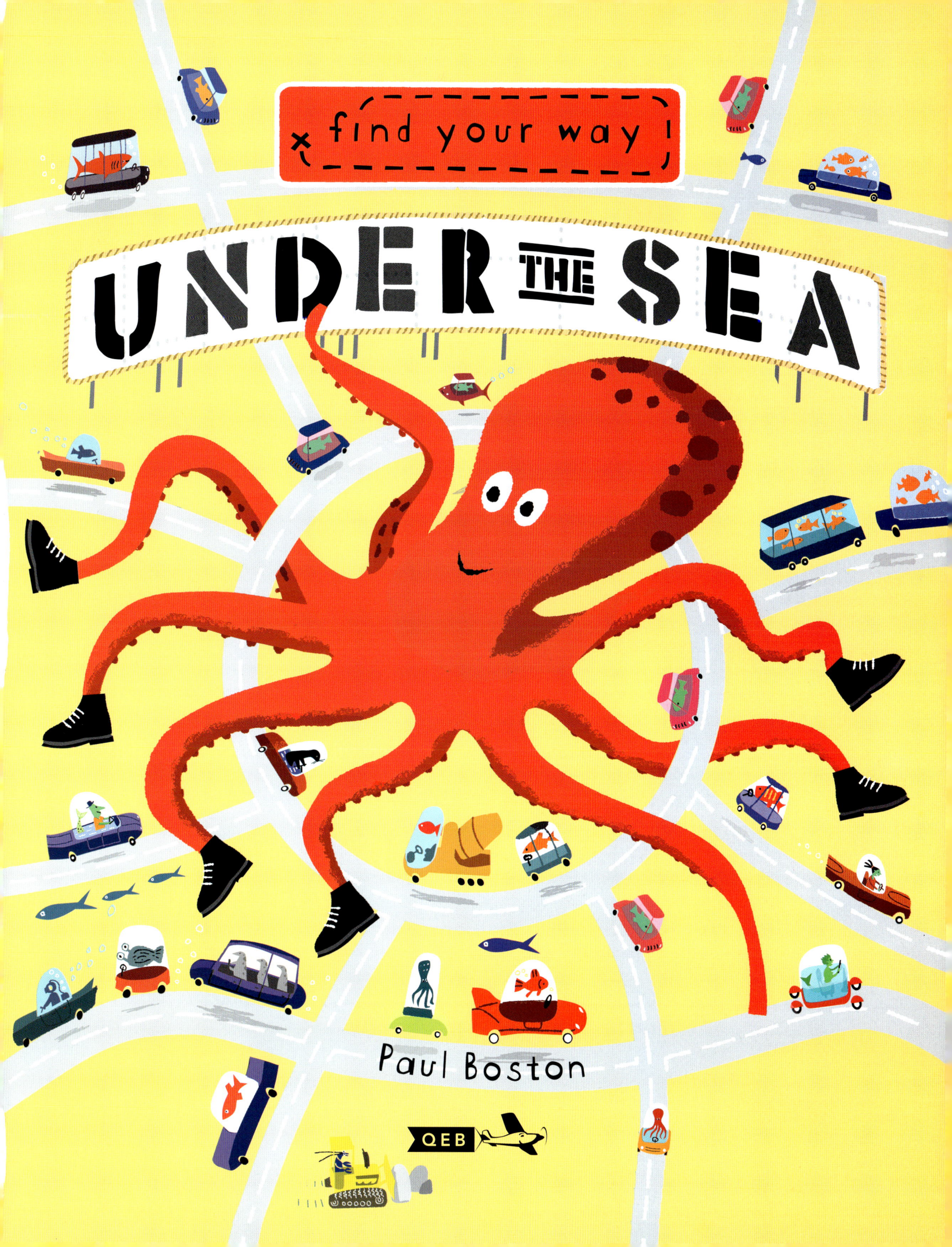

find your way
UNDER THE SEA

Paul Boston

QEB

YOUR MISSION

Welcome to Merp Town. We need your help to finish building our castle. Find your way there by choosing which exits or entrances to follow on each page.

1 Choose your transport

Submarine

Sea Turtle

Seahorse

2 Trace a route

There are lots to choose from and you can go **BACKWARD** and **FORWARD** along the same road.

3 Collect on every page

Choose ONE of the missions below to help the Merps. You will find one of each object in every scene.

Collect **12 SHINY PEARLS** to decorate the princess's bedroom.

Collect **12 BURGERS** for the hungry castle builders.

Collect **12 SHARK TEETH** to use as tools to help build the castle.

4 Use the book LIKE A REAL MAP

Turn the pages and use coordinates in this book just like you would with a real map. You can find out more about coordinates on pages 4 and 5.

5 Solve math puzzles

Along the way you will come across Merps who are lost or need your help. You will have to use your super math skills to help them. You might be asked to count up to ten or to find a shape.

Welcome to Merp Town

Look at the map of Merp Town. Can you see where the castle is? That's where you need to get to. Let's use coordinates to help us describe where the castle is on the map.

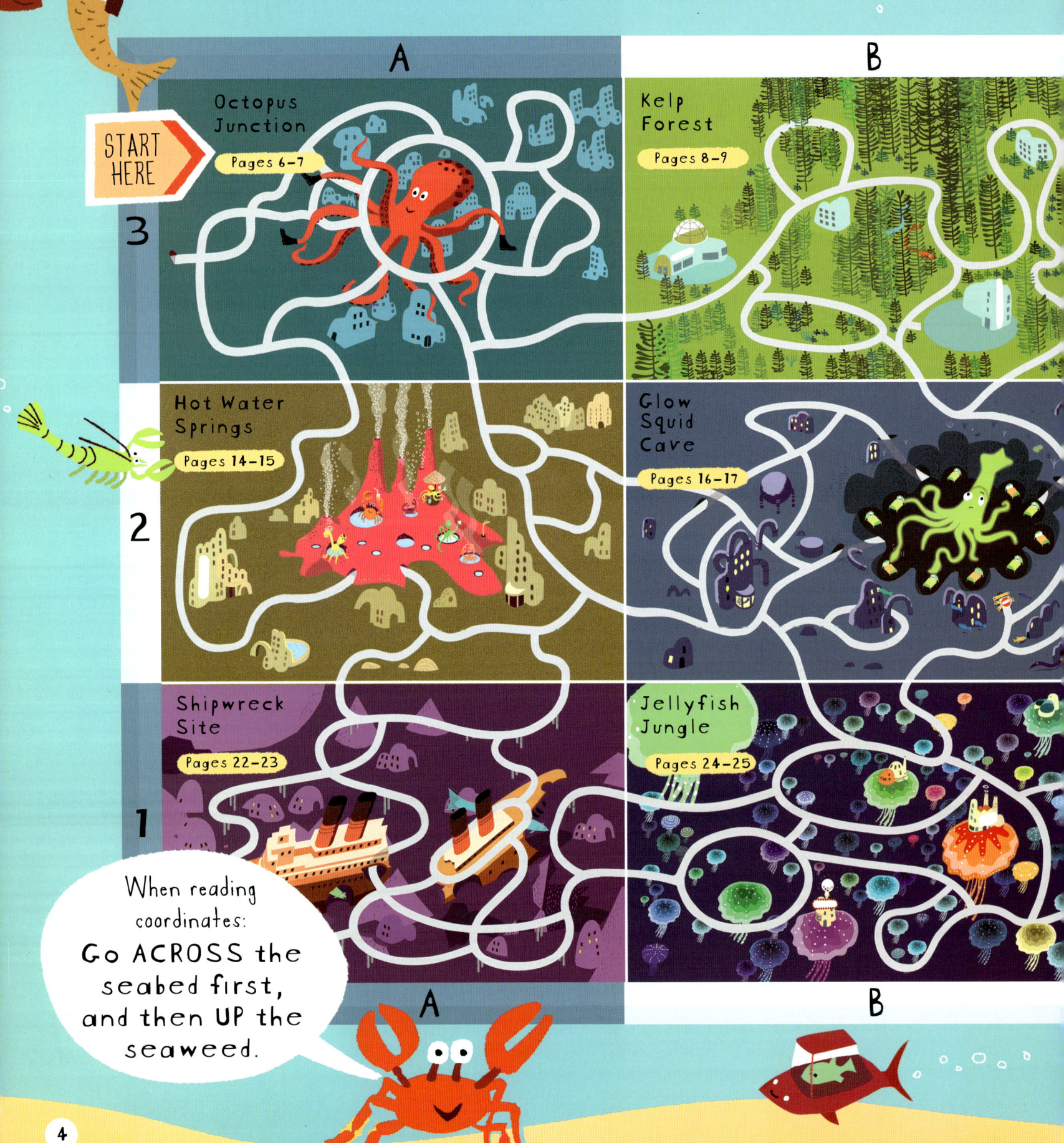

START HERE

A
- Octopus Junction — Pages 6-7
- Hot Water Springs — Pages 14-15
- Shipwreck Site — Pages 22-23

B
- Kelp Forest — Pages 8-9
- Glow Squid Cave — Pages 16-17
- Jellyfish Jungle — Pages 24-25

3, **2**, **1**

When reading coordinates: Go ACROSS the seabed first, and then UP the seaweed.

What are coordinates?

Coordinates are a set of letters and numbers that show where something is on a map. The letter comes first, followed by the number, so the castle is in (D,1). Look for the coordinate symbol throughout the book.

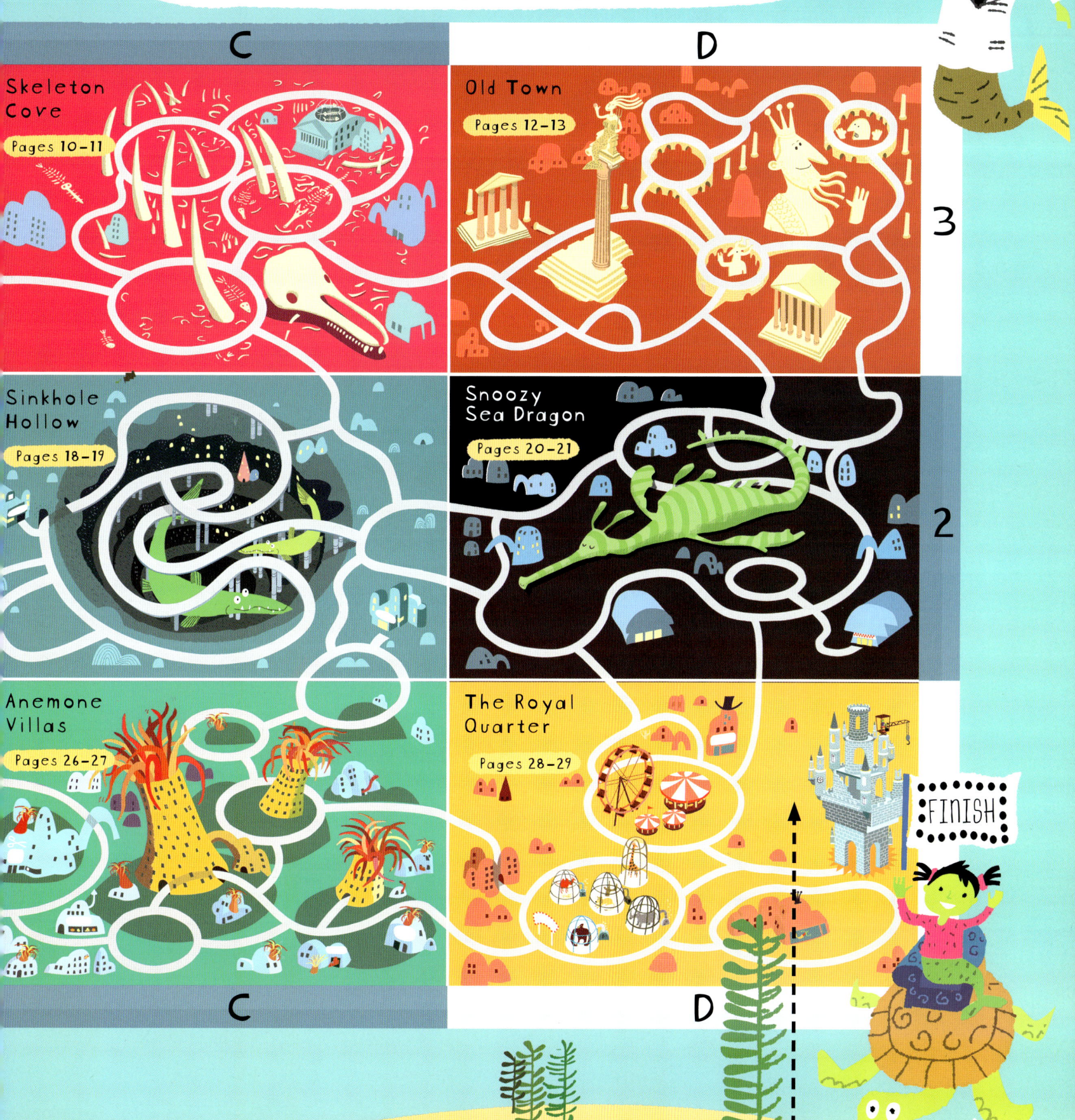

	C	D	
	Skeleton Cove Pages 10-11	**Old Town** Pages 12-13	3
	Sinkhole Hollow Pages 18-19	**Snoozy Sea Dragon** Pages 20-21	2
	Anemone Villas Pages 26-27	**The Royal Quarter** Pages 28-29	
	C	D	

FINISH

5

Oh no! Mr. Tentacles is blocking the way! Find a way around him to carry on with your mission. Use your finger to help. Can you spot your object anywhere?

- SHARK TOOTH
- BURGER
- PEARL

I'm lost! Can you please tell me the coordinates for the bank?

START HERE

OCTOPUS JUNCTION

Stop! Count how many shoes Mr. Tentacles is missing before I let you pass.

AQUA PETS

Go to page 14
HOT WATER SPRINGS

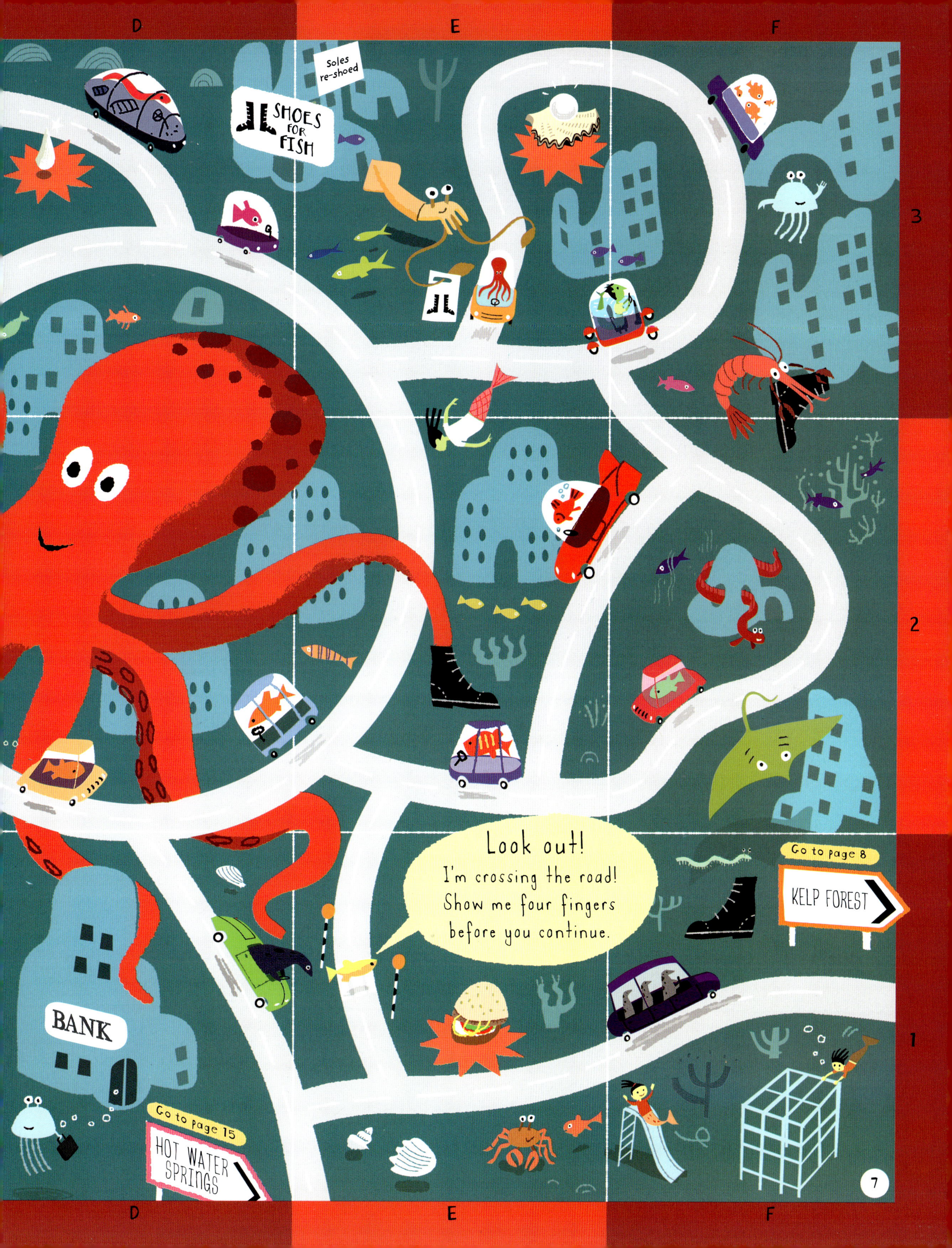
D
E
F
Soles re-shoed
SHOES FOR FISH
3
2
Look out!
I'm crossing the road!
Show me four fingers
before you continue.
Go to page 8
KELP FOREST
1
BANK
Go to page 15
HOT WATER SPRINGS
D
E
F

Welcome to Kelp Forest!

The plants here have grown very tall—some are as high as buildings! What can you see hiding between the leaves?

- SHARK TOOTH
- BURGER
- PEARL

How many books am I taking back to the library?

Go to page 7
OCTOPUS JUNCTION

KELP FOREST

Stop! The traffic lights are red! Count to ten before you continue.

D
E
F
I'm looking for the restaurant. Can you tell me which coordinates it is in?
3
2
1
Go to page 10
SKELETON COVE
RESTAURANT
Go to page 17
GLOW SQUID CAVE
Go to page 17
GLOW SQUID CAVE
D
E
F

Spooky! These are the bones of a dinosaur who lived in the sea millions of years ago. Lots of people come to visit. Can you find the crocodile skeleton? It's blocking the road.

SHARK TOOTH   BURGER   PEARL

I'm ten minutes late! If I should have met my wife at 11.30am, what time is it now?

Go to page 9
← KELP FOREST

SKELETON COVE

I am sure the coordinates of the skeleton gift shop were (C,1) but now I am lost. Can you help?

D
E
F
BONEY TOURS
MUSEUM
Hey! I'm crossing the road. You can continue if you finish this sequence: 2...4...6... ... ...
3
2
1
BONE SCHOOL
Go to page 12
OLD TOWN
SKELETON GIFT SHOP
Go to page 19
SINKHOLE HOLLOW
D
E
F

You've reached the Old Town!

There are lots of very old buildings and statues here. Drive around this ancient place to find your object.

- SHARK TOOTH
- BURGER
- PEARL

Which statue is the tallest?

OLD TOWN

Go to page 11
SKELETON COVE

TACOS

The traffic lights are yellow. Get ready in 3...2...1...stop!

D
E
F
3
2
1
We are on a school trip to the Art Gallery! Where is it?
ART GALLERY
Go to page 21
Snoozy Sea Dragon
Go to page 21
Snoozy Sea Dragon
D
E
F

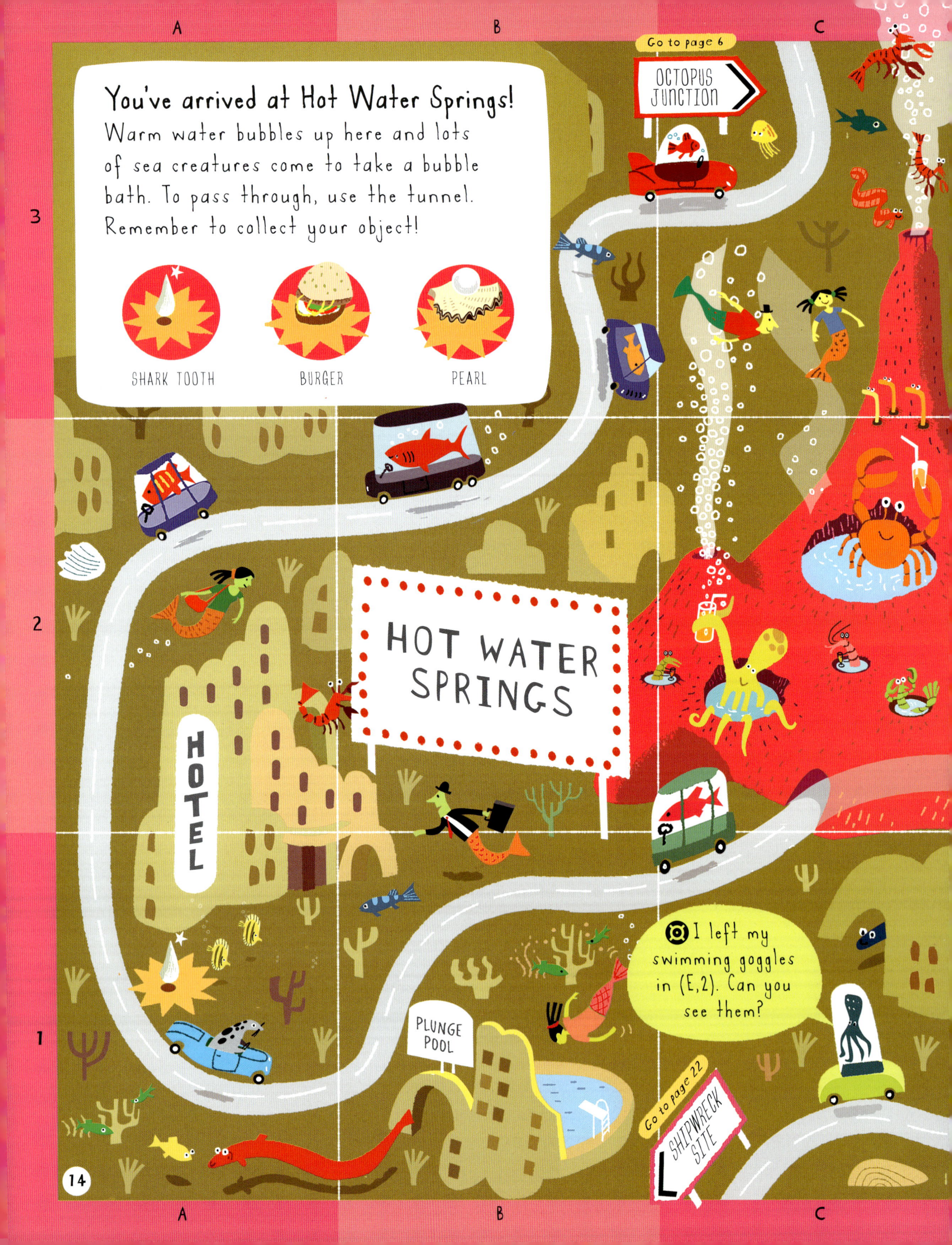

You've arrived at Hot Water Springs! Warm water bubbles up here and lots of sea creatures come to take a bubble bath. To pass through, use the tunnel. Remember to collect your object!

- SHARK TOOTH
- BURGER
- PEARL

Go to page 6
OCTOPUS JUNCTION

HOT WATER SPRINGS

HOTEL

PLUNGE POOL

I left my swimming goggles in (E,2). Can you see them?

Go to page 22
SHIPWRECK SITE

D
E
F
Go to page 7
OCTOPUS JUNCTION
Go to page 16
GLOW SQUID CAVE
3
Wait!
Someone is crossing the road. Show me seven fingers before you continue.
TOWN HALL
SPRINGS HOTEL
2
Go to page 16
GLOW SQUID CAVE
1
Go to page 23
SHIPWRECK SITE
This bus can only take six passengers. How many more will fit in?
D
E
F

Poor Mrs. Glow-Bottom has lost some of her babies! Count how many are missing. You might even spot some on your way.

- SHARK TOOTH
- BURGER
- PEARL

Go to page 15
HOT WATER SPRINGS

Go to page 15
HOT WATER SPRINGS

INK

GLOW SQUID CAVE

INK WORKS

TACOS

Special price for all red vehicles. How many can you count?

Hold on! The traffic lights are red! Show me ten fingers before you continue.

Go to page 24
JELLYFISH JUNGLE

Go to page 9
KELP FOREST >

< Go to page 9
KELP FOREST

Go to page 18
SINKHOLE HOLLOW >

Go to page 25
JELLYFISH JUNGLE

Watch your step! A huge hole has appeared in the ground and it is over 300 feet deep! Luckily, there are big, strong roads to help you travel across safely.

SHARK TOOTH   BURGER   PEARL

SINKHOLE HOLLOW

Go to page 17
GLOW SQUID CAVE

Can you please tell me where the school is?

18

D E F

Go to page 11
SKELETON COVE
Watch out!
We are crossing the road. Count to five before you continue.
I'm looking for the cone-shaped building. Can you see it? It is pink and has four windows.
Go to page 20
SNOOZY SEA DRAGON
Go to page 20
SNOOZY SEA DRAGON
SCHOOL
Go to page 27
ANEMONE VILLAS
Go to page 27
ANEMONE VILLAS

3
2
1

D E F

Uh oh! Snozzles the sea dragon has fallen asleep and is blocking the road! To continue collecting your object, you will have to travel around him. Shhh!

SHARK TOOTH   BURGER   PEARL

Go to page 19
SINKHOLE HOLLOW

Go to page 19
SINKHOLE HOLLOW

Can you please tell me the coordinates for the police station? It's an emergency!

ALL-NIGHT SUPERMARKET

Go to page 28
THE ROYAL QUARTER

D
E
F
Go to page 13
OLD TOWN
Go to page 13
OLD TOWN
3
How many policemen can you see in (B,2)?
Snoozy SEA DRAGON
2
POLICE
1
Go to page 29
THE ROYAL QUARTER
D
E
F

Welcome to the Shipwreck Site!
This old ruin was once a ship, which crashed and sunk to the bottom of the sea. It is too big to move, so the Merps have cleverly made tunnels through it.

SHARK TOOTH   BURGER   PEARL

Go to page 14
HOT WATER SPRINGS ▶

Where is the treasure chest? I'm going to be rich! Yippee!

D
E
F
Go to page 15
HOT WATER SPRINGS
SHIPWRECK SITE
Oh dear. I should have started work at 9am. It's now 9:15. How late am I?
Go to page 24
JELLYFISH JUNGLE
Go to page 24
JELLYFISH JUNGLE
3
2
1
D
E
F

Wow! Look at all these jellyfish! They have come here because there is lots of their favorite food around, plankton. Pass through slowly to find your object.

- SHARK TOOTH
- BURGER
- PEARL

Go to page 16
GLOW SQUID CAVE

I'm taking my children to the candy factory! Where is it?

Go to page 23
SHIPWRECK SITE

Go to page 23
SHIPWRECK SITE

JELLYFISH JUNGLE

TOFFEE SHOP

Which building can you see in (C,1)?

24

D
E
F
Go to page 17
GLOW SQUID CAVE
Can you find a yellow jellyfish with five orange spots?
Jelly worms
3
Go to page 26
ANEMONE VILLAS
Fizzy Sherbet
CANDY FACTORY
2
Go to page 26
ANEMONE VILLAS
1
D
E
F

You have reached Anemone Villas!

Lots of Merps live here. Be careful not to get too close to the tentacles as you look for your object as they can sting!

- SHARK TOOTH
- BURGER
- PEARL

Go to page 25
JELLYFISH JUNGLE

Hair Cuts

Which anemone building is the biggest?

Go to page 25
JELLYFISH JUNGLE

Bakery

ANEMONE VILLAS

Go to page 19
SINKHOLE HOLLOW

Go to page 19
SINKHOLE HOLLOW

I'm hungry! Where can I find somewhere that sells cakes?

Go to page 28
THE ROYAL QUARTER

Wait! The traffic lights are red. Clap ten times before you continue.

Go to page 28
THE ROYAL QUARTER

ANEMONE CAFE

Noodles

27

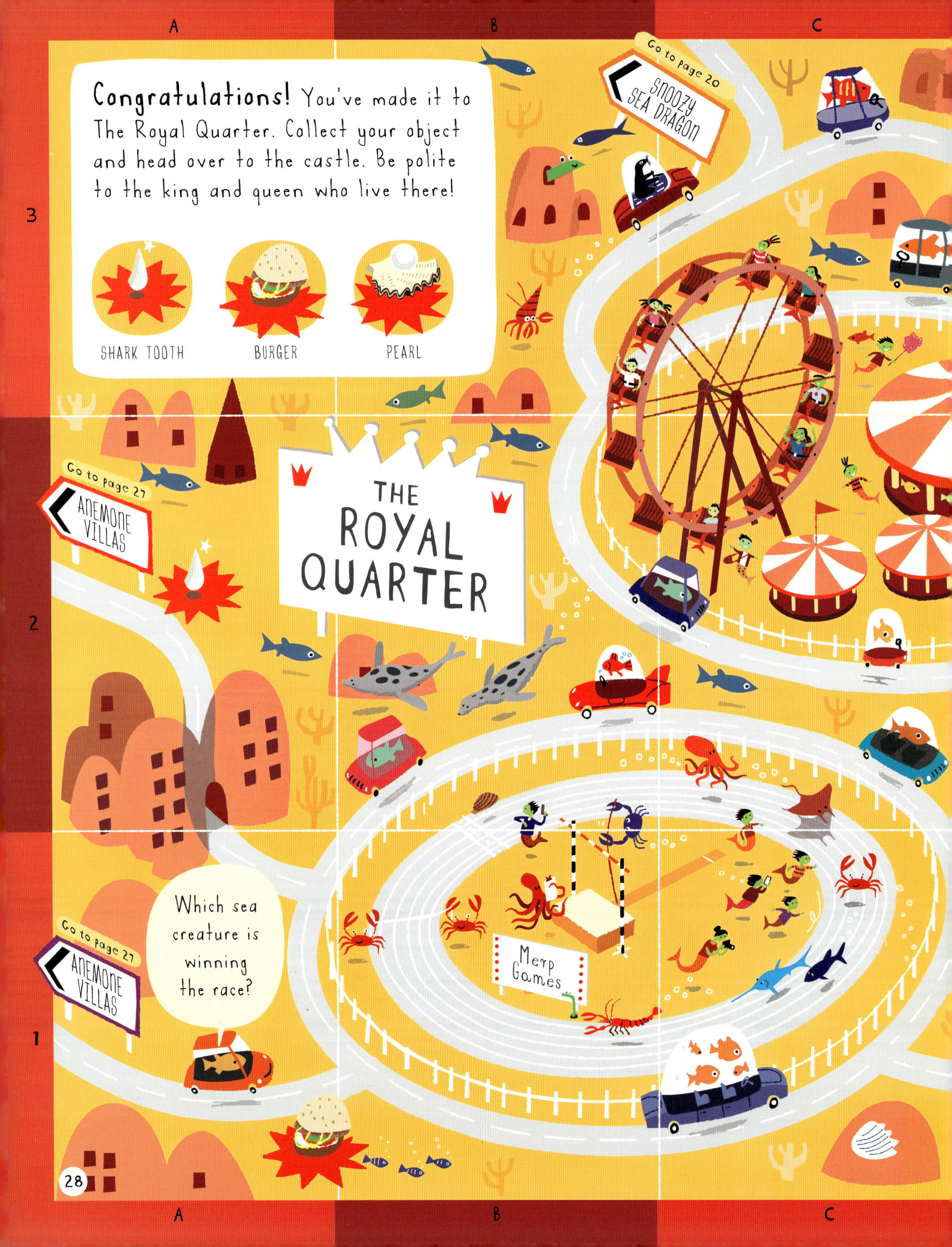

Congratulations! You've made it to The Royal Quarter. Collect your object and head over to the castle. Be polite to the king and queen who live there!

SHARK TOOTH · BURGER · PEARL

Go to page 20
SNOOZY SEA DRAGON

THE ROYAL QUARTER

Go to page 27
ANEMONE VILLAS

Go to page 27
ANEMONE VILLAS

Which sea creature is winning the race?

Merp Games

28

D
E
F
Go to page 21
SNOOZY SEA DRAGON
HATS
3
Hooray, you're here! Travel through the main gates and then turn the page...
MERP CASTLE
2
Royal Fashions
I want to buy a new hat. Where should I go?
1
D
E
F

Does the green starfish have five arms or six?

Are there more red flags than blue flags?

Can you find the circular window? Who is inside it?

PRINCESS BEDROOM

KITCHEN

Well done! You have completed your mission successfully and are inside the castle! Can you find the king, queen, and princess? They will tell you what to do with your objects.

There are three places in the castle that need decorating with pearls. Find each place and fill in the holes.
One burger each please! We're hungry!
BANQUET HALL
The twelve builders in red jackets are ready for lunch. Please give one burger to each of them.
GARAGE
Climb the longest ladder, and then the longest rope and give your shark teeth to the twelve builders in yellow jackets.
Go and say hello to Mr. Seal by the top floor!

MORE FUN UNDER THE SEA!

Understanding Coordinates
Encourage your child to look at other places where they might find coordinates, such as on an A-Z map. Draw a pirate's map together and plan your route to the treasure, or play a game of Battleships.

Counting
Go back through the book and look for more opportunities to encourage counting under the sea. How many arms does an octopus have? How many claws does a crab have?

Telling the Time
Make a simple clock with your child to encourage them to look closely at telling the time. Use a paper plate, and attach arms using a metal fastener or chenille stems. You could even decorate it to look like a turtle. Fill in the clock face using colored pens. To go a step further, make paper "flaps" which can be lifted up to reveal the minutes.

Recognizing Shapes
Make a sea monster! Cut out lots of different 2D shapes from colored paper. You could use triangles for the flippers, a circle for the body, and squares for its scales. What shape would its teeth be? You could even try making 3D shapes from modeling clay.

Math Problems and Vocabulary
Go back through the book and look for opportunities to build on mathematics vocabulary and problem solving skills. For example, what is the total number of baby squid? Or, if there are three jellyfish with ten legs each, how many legs are there altogether?

Measurements
Using building blocks, make a little underwater town with your child. Can you make a really tall block of apartments like the Anemone Villas? What about a long boat or a short submarine?

Quarto is the authority on a wide range of topics.
Quarto educates, entertains and enriches the lives of our readers—enthusiasts and lovers of hands-on living.
www.quartoknows.com

Written and edited by: Joanna McInerney and the QED team
Designed by: Mike Henson
Consultant: Alistair Bryce-Clegg

Copyright © QEB Publishing 2016

First published in the United States by
QEB Publishing, Inc.
6 Orchard
Lake Forest, CA 92630

All rights reserved. No part of this publication may be reproduced, stored in a retrieval system, or transmitted in any form or by any means, electronic, mechanical, photocopying, recording, or otherwise, without the prior permission of the publisher, nor be otherwise circulated in any form of binding or cover other than that in which it is published and without a similar condition being imposed on the subsequent purchaser.

A catalog record for this book is available from the Library of Congress.

ISBN 978 1 68297 034 8

Printed in China